Original title:
Tall Tales from Tiny Trees

Copyright © 2025 Creative Arts Management OÜ
All rights reserved.

Author: Ethan Prescott
ISBN HARDBACK: 978-1-80567-393-4
ISBN PAPERBACK: 978-1-80567-692-8

Whispers of the Little Giants

In the shadow of the tiny pine,
Squirrels wear hats, sipping wine.
They toast to leaves with silly cheers,
As holey acorns dance with peers.

The ant parade is quite a sight,
Carrying crumbs beneath moonlight.
With little drums, they march in line,
The tiny trees, their grand design.

Secrets in the Shrubs

Behind the bushes, jokes unfold,
A hedgehog tells tales, bright and bold.
With every quill, a story spins,
Of lost socks and where the fun begins.

The rabbits giggle, play charades,
As fireflies light up the glades.
Their laughter echoes through the night,
In the world of shrubs, all feels right.

The Chronicles of the Miniature Forest

Tiny mushrooms, dressed so fine,
Host a ball for vines and twine.
They waltz beneath the starry skies,
With twinkling lights in their eyes.

The critters gather, all in pairs,
Telling secrets, sharing cares.
A beetle juggles pebbles and leaves,
In this forest, joy never leaves.

Legends of the Lilliputian Woods

In the woods where laughter grows,
The tiny trees hide funny shows.
A gnome named Fred rides on a snail,
While tales are spun from every trail.

The ladybugs play bingo games,
Chasing after wiggly flames.
With every win, they cheer and sing,
In this small world, joy's the king.

Mirth in the Miniature Orchard

In a grove where the apples glow,
A squirrel claims he runs the show.
He tries to juggle pears, oh dear!
But they splat on his head, what a cheer!

Tiny peaches dance in the breeze,
While giggling branches sway with ease.
A mouse in overalls, full of flair,
Leads a parade with not a care!

Tales of the Dwarfing Oak

Once an oak thought he was grand,
With a trunk so thick, it took a stand.
Until he saw a twig in bloom,
Said, "I need a ladder to clear this room!"

He hosted a party, short and sweet,
With acorns bouncing to the beat.
A raccoon DJ spun some tunes,
While rabbits boogied under the moon!

Legends of the Little Leaf

A little leaf with a big, bold dream,
Sought to conquer the sunlight beam.
He climbed a branch, oh what a sight,
But the wind said, "Buddy, you're quite light!"

His friends cheered him, all a-flutter,
As he tangled with a passing butter.
Then he twirled down with such a flair,
Landed soft on a hedgehog's hair!

Chronicles of the Twinkling Sprouts

Sprouts with boots tap danced on soil,
Wearing hats made from last year's foil.
They giggled loud at their own tricks,
As worms rolled in laughter, doing flips.

In the nighttime, they threw a bash,
While fireflies lit up the splash.
With silly songs, they'd proudly sing,
Of how they found a lost old ring!

Vignettes from the Verdant Realm

In a garden where gnomes do play,
A squirrel tells jokes by the bay.
The daisies chuckle, the roses grin,
As the sun shines down, let the fun begin.

A hedgehog in spectacles reads quite loud,
To a gathering of mushrooms, a curious crowd.
The ferns jiggle lightly, all wrapped in green,
While a rabbit prances, proud and keen.

Each pine tree sways, joining the song,
With whispers of mischief, they all get along.
The acorns giggle and slip on the dew,
Making a splash as the day's fun ensues.

So gather round, let laughter unfurl,
In this world of green, every fable's a whirl.
With a wink and a nod, tales dart to the sky,
In this verdant realm, we'll laugh till we cry.

The Whispering Shrubs' Refrain

Under the shade of a chuckling beech,
A crabapple whispers, with humor to teach.
The breezes giggle, swaying the leaves,
As the willows weave in their breezy thieves.

A raccoon in boots, on a mission so grand,
Bids farewell to the beetles, who form an old band.
With a tap of their shells, they dance with delight,
As the moon spills laughter into the night.

The lilac blooms burst with colors so bright,
While the daisies argue who's the prettiest sight.
The sun dips low, pulling shadows so sly,
As crickets compose a tune in the sky.

With the chirps and the funny tales shared so well,
Every leaf has a secret, every stem has a spell.
In this garden of giggles, come join for a chat,
Where humor grows wildly—imagine that!

Petal-Powered Legends

In a garden where daisies dance,
Butterflies wear their finest pants,
A sunflower sings in a breezy tune,
While crickets juggle by the light of the moon.

The roses gossip, oh what a show,
About the daffodils, in a row,
Lilies pretend they're fashion queens,
With petals dripping in sweet, silly scenes.

A gnome grins, holding a tiny mug,
Tales of bees that play and hug,
And ants that race on pebble lanes,
Spinning yarns of their tiny gains.

The moon chuckles, shining so bright,
As saplings plot their pranks at night,
With whispers and giggles from every tree,
In a world where size means little glee.

The Secret Life of Shrubs

Beneath the hedge, a party blooms,
With chatting bushes in little rooms,
A hedgehog DJ spins the beat,
As squirrels stomp their tiny feet.

The lilac throws a color show,
While roses crack jokes about dandelions' glow,
The tall hedges tell of windy tales,
Of leaves that sail like tiny gales.

In bushes, secrets get swapped and shared,
Of thorns that flaunt how much they've dared,
While bunnies laugh at the prickly crew,
Plans for mischief in the morning dew.

With branches sway and rustling leaves,
The shrubs weave stories that no one believes,
As fireflies blink in the dark, quite spry,
Underneath the stars, friendships never die.

Heartbeats Beneath the Bark

In the forest, whispers flow,
From critters beneath, down below,
A woodpecker's drumbeat starts a tune,
Echoed by owls in a light-hearted croon.

Trees lend ears to the tales of old,
Where squirrels stake claims on treasures untold,
While mushrooms play dice with a charming glee,
Over acorn bets and their cozy tea.

With roots that tap dance, they tease the ground,
Spinning stories of magic found,
Of glimmering stones and bubblegum trees,
That giggle and wiggle in the softest breeze.

As moonlight spills on this symphony,
Even the grumpy rocks join in glee,
With heartbeats thrumming beneath the bark,
Making legends that sing till it's dark.

Whims of the Whittle Woods

In Whittle Woods, the trees have fun,
Racing the clouds, they can almost run,
Spruce sprigs giggle, as they tag each other,
While poplar shoots leap like they're from their mother.

With branches swaying like a dance floor,
The elms tell tales of a hairy bore,
As bushes bluff about limbs that twist,
In competitions no one can resist.

In the shade, chipmunks drape in flair,
Wearing acorn hats, they don't have a care,
While crickets boast of their leggy might,
With battles wrung in the moon's soft light.

The woods are alive, where laughter's free,
With every nook bursting at the sea,
In this whimsical place where dreams abide,
Tiny wonders play, with joy and pride.

Stories of the Shortened Timber

In a forest where squirrels wear hats,
Lived a tree who dreamt of chubby chats.
He made friends with weeds and tiny ants,
Together they leaped in funny pants.

The robins laughed, the crickets sung,
For every branch was just a lung.
They whispered secrets to the moon,
And danced around a thimble's tune.

A stump told legends of grasshopper kings,
With crowns made of acorns, oh what bling!
They fought fierce battles with leaves as shields,
Laughing so hard, the laughter yields.

In the shade, they played games of charades,
While the sun peeked through leafy cascades.
Oh, short timber tales, such grandeur indeed,
In a world where all flourish, plant a seed!

The Tryst of Tiny Twigs

Two twigs met beneath a grand old bough,
Each claiming to be the finest, oh wow!
They danced in circles, a sight to adore,
But one tripped and fell, shouting for more!

The neighbors, a band of bustling bees,
Buzzed with laughter, amusing with glee.
They declared a contest of who was the best,
A sprightly event, a lively fest!

From the dirt, they crafted tiny crowns,
Out of fluff and fluff, and bits of browndowns.
But when they wore them, they both took flight,
And landed in mud, what a silly sight!

Yet twigs are tricky and don't hold a grudge,
They hugged it out, though both felt the smudge.
In laughter, they found their perfect groove,
Sharing their tangle in a playful move!

Myths of Moonlit Meadows

In moonlit meadows, shadows twist,
Grass tickles feet of the fluffy mist.
A weasel told tales of the old, wise snail,
Whose wisdom was lost in a grand detail.

The stars giggled as the owl wore a hat,
While the rabbits debated on who was fat.
A dance broke out, led by a firefly,
Who twinkled and flaunted as he zipped by.

Mice held a feast with crumbs of delight,
Underneath mushrooms that glowed in the night.
Each crumb was a story, each bite was a laugh,
In a meadow where we shared a hearty half.

When dawn broke, the tales turned to mist,
Leaving behind the laughter, they couldn't resist.
For in the moonlight, they discovered the glee,
Of sharing wild myths in a bright jubilee!

Echoes of the Elfin Arbor

In a grove where the elves often weave,
Mischief and giggles are hard to believe.
They toss tiny berries like cannonballs,
And chase each other with gnome-sized brawls.

The trees listen close to the raucous fun,
As mushrooms grow large under the sun.
An acorn declared, 'I'll be the king!'
But tripped on a root while trying to swing.

Frogs croaked tales of the jumpiest crew,
And the dragonfly zoomed, oh how he flew!
In that tiny world where the laughter erupted,
Every small soul felt vastly disrupted.

As the sun set, the forest turned bright,
With echoes of laughter as charms took flight.
In the elfin arbor, the stories won't tire,
Each giggle a spark, an ever-lit fire!

The Enchanted Espalier

In the garden there's a vine,
Climbing up and looking fine.
With a wink it sways just so,
Whispering secrets, 'Watch me grow!'

Beneath its leaves, a gnome resides,
With wild tales and wobbly rides.
Every berry tells a joke,
As giggles from the branches broke.

Oh, the bees wear tiny hats,
And dance around like acrobats.
With every buzz, a laughter swells,
In the tale of the tree, who tells?

So join the fun in sun's warm rays,
Where every branch in laughter plays.
This espaliers' a happy chap,
In leafy curls, we find our map.

Secrets of the Shrubbery Champions

In the bushes where snickers grow,
A champion shrub puts on its show.
With leafy limbs that twist and twirl,
It claims to be the mightiest girl.

The daisies laugh with giddy glee,
In whispers soft, 'Just look and see!'
For when the moonlight takes its flight,
The shrub tells tales that ignite the night.

'I've won at hide and seek!' it claims,
While butterflies play silly games.
Their giggles paint the evening air,
For secrets here are rare and fair.

So if you wander past this place,
Keep an ear for the shrub's embrace.
It's a champion with crafty roots,
And shares its tales in leafy hoots.

Ballads of the Bewitched Bark

There's a tree with bark so wise,
It tells of pigeons, clouds, and skies.
With every knot, a tale unfolds,
Of little adventures, bravely told.

A squirrel once asked for a yarn,
And the tree replied, 'I'll never scorn!
For swinging high, and jumping low,
You'll find the magic, if you know!'

So listen close to rustling leaves,
As laughter dances, and joy achieves.
The ballads weave through branches wide,
And every creature joins the ride.

Frogs in hats tap a lively beat,
As crickets chirp, oh what a treat!
The bark has seen the sun and dark,
And in its heart, it holds a spark.

The Saga of the Small Seeds

A tiny seed with dreams galore,
Hopped away, one sleepy morn.
It whispered low, 'I can't be small,
I'll grow up high, right to the ball!'

In a flower pot named Mr. High,
The seed was sure it would touch the sky.
With every sprout it swirled around,
And made the wildest sounds profound.

A ladybug sang a sweet refrain,
While ants clapped feet like an endless train.
Each petal danced, each leaf took flight,
In this saga of silly delight.

So watch the seeds, they're never mild,
For in each soul, there grows a child.
With giggles shared in every deed,
The funniest stories from tiny seed!

Wonders of the Woodland Sprite

A sprite once danced on a mushroom hat,
She taught a squirrel to wear a spat.
With acorn cups and berries neat,
They threw a party, it was quite the feat.

The owls played music with a howling tune,
While raccoons twirled beneath the moon.
Tiny friends on a log did glide,
What a sight, a joyful ride!

The mushrooms chuckled, the trees swayed low,
As laughter echoed from below.
A sprite with flair and a giggle tight,
Left all the critters in pure delight.

So if you wander by the old oak tree,
Listen closely, you might see,
A dance of joy, a woodland cheer,
Where sprites and critters spread the cheer!

Secrets of the Verdant Shadows

In the shadows where secrets hide,
A chubby hedgehog took a slide.
Down a mossy hill he rolled and spun,
With a laugh so deep, oh what fun!

The ferns waved like hands in glee,
As bunnies joined in for a spree.
With every tumble, every twist,
They left behind a fuzzy mist.

A wise old owl watched from above,
He hooted softly, sharing love.
The secrets whispered among the trees,
Became a chorus of playful pleas.

So venture forth, where shadows lay,
Find the fun in nature's play.
The secrets of laughter, wild and free,
Are waiting for you, come join the spree!

Parables of the Pint-Sized Pines

Pint-sized pines with branches small,
Held meetings where they'd gaily sprawl.
They spoke of dreams, of clouds so high,
While squirrels practiced a silly fly.

The acorns laughed with little chimes,
Reciting gags from ancient times.
A tiny pine told a joke so grand,
Even the stones couldn't help but stand.

With each hearty laugh, the breeze would sigh,
As butterflies danced and drifted by.
A parable told of a wise old bee,
Who buzzed around, as happy as can be.

So gather 'round and hear the cheer,
From nature's wisdom, let's all draw near.
In the dance of pines and acorns round,
The joy of life is always found!

Whimsies in the Woodlands

In the woodlands where whimsy grows,
A rabbit stole a gnome's old hose.
He watered flowers with a grin,
Making them bloom with a twirl and spin.

The fairies giggled, balloons in hand,
Creating bubbles that floated and spanned.
Each burst a pop, a tickling sound,
Chasing critters all around.

A fox wore glasses, looking quite spry,
Counting stars in the night sky.
With each twinkle, he'd make a wish,
For funny tales and a dancing fish.

So wander forth, let joy align,
In woodlands where the laughter's fine.
Join the whimsy, let your heart free,
In this grand forest, come dance and be!

Sagas from the Shrubby Heights

In a bush, a rabbit wears a tie,
He holds court with squirrels passing by.
They claim that grasshoppers can sing,
While crickets debate who's the hardest thing.

A snail tells tales of days so long,
That ants applaud with little songs.
They huddle close beneath the glow,
Of glowworms who dance in a row.

A hedgehog with a crown of leaves,
Believes he's king, oh how he deceives!
His royal court, a motley crew,
Of beetles that chuckle and flies that boo.

As shadows lengthen and giggles rise,
The tiny trees whisper their funny lies.
In the heart of the meadow, adventure thrives,
Amongst the tiny tales and munching lives.

Miniature Marvels in the Meadow

A grass blade hosts a tiny feast,
Where mice dance like they're the least.
With acorn hats and tiny shoes,
They boogie down with no time to lose.

Fireflies light the waltzing scene,
As ladybugs cheer like they're on screen.
A worm in a tux takes center stage,
While daisies turn the next page.

Under the moon, a wild parade,
Of hopping frogs, their joy displayed.
In tiny hearts, laughter springs,
Making the meadow burst with wings.

The night hums soft with chuckling cheer,
As even the crickets lend an ear.
In this little world, dreams take flight,
With the humor that sparkles through the night.

Chronicles of the Compact Canopy

In a nook, the owls spin golden yarn,
Of foxes who play tricks in the barn.
With whispers soft as the breeze that sways,
They share murmurs of mischief-filled days.

Beneath the branches, the whispers flow,
Of a turtle with a big heart who steals the show.
He claims to run in the time of dreams,
But everyone knows he's slower than beams.

A family of mice put on a play,
Reenacting picnics from the sunny day.
Each act is more twisted than the last,
With crumbs and giggles from the past.

Amidst the leaves, laughter does bloom,
Inviting all into the cozy room.
The canopy knows how to keep a secret right,
In this miniature world, we find pure delight.

The Leafy Lore of Little Places

From acorns sprout stories so bright,
Of chubby chipmunks that take flight.
They ride on feathers from the bluebirds,
And relish in the tales they've heard.

A woodpecker pens a comical tune,
That echoes sweetly 'neath the moon.
His drumming leads a feathery crowd,
Who gather round, excited, proud.

Bumblebees wear tiny goggles, you see,
As they race through the air like glee.
Their buzzing jokes make blossoms sway,
As petals giggle at the display.

In these little nooks, the laughter is found,
With antics unfolding all around.
The lore of green, with humor in grace,
Unveils the magic of this small space.

Fantasies in the Shade

Beneath a leaf, a frog wears a crown,
He rules the bugs in this tiny town.
With a wave of his hand, he casts out fear,
Sending crickets dancing, oh what a cheer!

A squirrel in a jacket plays violin,
The acorns clap along with a grin.
While a snail in shades slides down the bark,
Each note echoes bright, lighting up the park.

Under the ferns, the ants throw a bash,
With crumbs of breadcrumbs all gathered in a stash.
They serve tiny tea in thimbles so neat,
While beetles play chess and shuffle their feet.

As the sun sets low, they all sing a tune,
Celebrating life beneath the green moon.
In their small kingdom, joy knows no limits,
Where laughter thrives and life feels like a gimmick.

Adventures in the Arbor

A raccoon in goggles flies high on a kite,
He takes to the skies, oh what a sight!
With a string of white clouds trailing behind,
He sings to the wind, joyfully unconfined.

Little woodpeckers in capes zoom around,
Turning the treetops into battlegrounds.
With beaks like arrows, they dive and they soar,
Each mighty peck echoes—what's behind that door?

A chubby chipmunk, a hero in his town,
Saves lost acorns, never once wears a frown.
Each nut stored safely, a treasure divine,
He shares his stash with the squirrels over wine.

At dusk, all the critters gather to feast,
Beneath the stars, they dance—never a least.
With stories exchanged and laughter that grows,
In this woodland dance, everyone's a pro.

The Magic of Minuscule Woodlands

In a wee forest, a pixie plays tricks,
Covering mushrooms with sprinkles and licks.
With giggles and giggles, she sprinkles her dust,
Making toadstools bounce, oh what a must!

A hedgehog in rainboots jogs down the lane,
Splashing in puddles, he laughs out loud—what a gain!
Chasing his shadow, he races the sun,
In his world of bliss, there's always more fun.

Frogs tell tall stories, but oh what a twist,
Each tale is richer with a bit of mist.
With a flip and a flop, they leap through the air,
As the fireflies cheer, lighting up everywhere.

In the heart of this grove, surprise is the key,
Where every branch whispers, "Come join the spree!"
With mirth all around, no gloom in the glade,
These tiny woods hold secrets that never will fade.

Visions from the Verdant Visage

A curious caterpillar wears stylish clogs,
Strolling through lilies, he befriends some dogs.
They play leapfrog over dandelion seams,
Chasing butterflies' laughter in whimsical dreams.

An elder tree tells tales of the wind,
In his gnarled roots, old friendships begin.
With every crack in his bark, there's a tale,
Of a snail who once tried to ride a train's trail.

A pair of owls in spectacles read,
The latest gossip from a fallen seed.
They chuckle and hoot, spinning yarns we adore,
While throwing their wisdom just like confetti galore.

As the moon rises high, a concert of mates,
With crickets and frogs, they celebrate states.
In this brimming patch of green, full of smiles,
Life in these woods stretches out for miles.

Giants Beneath the Green

In the shade of a flower pot,
A giant fell asleep, oh what a spot!
His dreams were of candy, and skies so blue,
But woke up to find squirrels stealing his shoe.

A worm with a crown asked him to dance,
While ants started marching, giving a glance,
They pranced and they twirled, oh what a sight,
The giant just chuckled, feeling delight.

The grass whispered secrets, quite silly and wild,
While daisies painted faces on each little child,
They laughed at the clouds, who were passing by,
Singing off-key, as they floated high.

So next time you're walking near trees oh so great,
Remember the giants and their quirky fate,
For in every small thing, a story's tucked tight,
Like a gnome wearing shorts, what a comical sight!

Tales from the Twisted Roots

Beneath twisted roots where the shadows grow,
The fairies host parties with snacks all aglow.
Their laughter erupts like a tickling breeze,
As beetles do ballet with glittery knees.

A tree trunk decided it'd try to be tall,
But just stretched and cracked and then started to fall,
With a thud and a chuckle, it landed quite flat,
Now it's a big bench, and the bugs tip their hat.

The owls tell stories by moonlight so bright,
Of raccoons in capes who take off in the night,
While everyone giggles at the mischief they make,
Selling cookies to kids by the old garden lake.

So listen closely when the night starts to hum,
Of twisted tales from roots, oh what a fun drum!
For in every odd corner, a secret resides,
Of laughter and fun where imagination hides.

The Little Legends of Leafy Tales

In a patch of green grass where ants formed a band,
They played little fiddles and sang hand in hand,
A ladybug danced, a sight oh so sweet,
While a grasshopper drummed on a pebble for beat.

The trees shared tall gossip, all twisted and fun,
Of how the sun plays peek-a-boo with everyone,
And mushrooms debated the secrets they know,
Laughing at shadows with a whimsical glow.

A tiny old turtle with glasses quite round,
Told stories of pizzas from the sky that he found,
He spoke of a pizza, with toppings galore,
As the crowd roared with laughter, they begged him for more.

So if you find magic in bushes or grass,
Remember the legends that tickle and pass,
For even the smallest of things up to size,
Hold tales full of giggles beneath sunny skies.

Enigma of the Shrinking Canopy

In the canopy high where the monkeys debate,
Was a riddle of joy that they couldn't quite state,
'Why did the pinecone refuse to come down?
Because it thought it was wearing a crown!'

A squirrel wore socks with pretty polka dots,
Said he was the king of the terracotta pots,
He juggled some acorns while dancing a jig,
And everyone laughed, oh what a big gig!

The clouds had a giggle, tickled by breeze,
As they turned into shapes, like a monstrous cheese,
A joke on the ground, with laughter that swells,
Of a tree on a skateboard, oh what a tale tells!

So heed all the whispers that flutter up high,
For in every leaf, there's a wink from the sky,
Of silliness soaring through branches and twigs,
In a world that delights, with laughter and wigs!

Journey Through the Minuscule Grove

In the grove where the acorns play,
The squirrels wear hats made of hay.
They dance on the branches so sprightly,
Yelling, "We're nuts, and we're mighty!"

A ladybug rides on a twirling leaf,
Singing a song, causing disbelief.
With a wiggle and jiggle, she takes to the sky,
While the ants shout, "Hey, look at her fly!"

Among the mushrooms, a party unfolds,
With tiny umbrellas and stories retold.
They sip on dew drops and cheerfully laugh,
As the gnome takes a tumble, oh what a gaffe!

Now come take a peek in this whimsical scene,
Where every small creature is lively and keen.
The jokes and the laughter take off with a swirl,
In this minuscule grove, where mischief does whirl!

The Garden Gnome Chronicles

In the garden, the gnomes take a stand,
With spades in their hands, they're quite unplanned.
One jumps in a pot, oh what a sight,
Claiming, "I'm cooking up mischief tonight!"

A flower pot launched turned skyward with glee,
While a gnome yelled, "Oh, look! I can fly like a bee!"
They slip on the petals and glide on the grass,
As they giggle and tumble, the moments won't pass.

With hitches and hiccups, each prank is a blast,
Making puns about mushrooms, a friend from the past.
Under the moonlight, they share their tall tales,
Mixing giggles with gigabytes, oh, how it prevails!

And as the sun rises, they stretch in delight,
Winking at bugs who buzz by in flight.
This garden of gnomes is nothing but cheer,
Creating their legends, year after year!

The Enigma of the Little Conifers

In a forest of whispers, the conifers stand,
With their branches all tickled by a mischievous hand.
One claims it's a treehouse where fairies convene,
While a pinecone argues, "Nah, it's just me and my bean!"

The spruce starts to giggle, it's a hilarious sight,
Saying, "We're just tiny, but we're still full of might!"
They toss down their needles like confetti and cheer,
As the saplings gather for a bonkers good year!

With whispers of wisdom, they share with the breeze,
Tales of the acorns and their crazy expertise.
"Dare we build castles from mounds of soft moss?"
And laughter erupts, treating worries like dross!

So under the canopy, the joy multiplies,
As these little conifers bask in their size.
With secrets and jest, they're bound to agree,
The magic of mischief is wondrous, you see!

Tiny Tales in the Lush Blue

In the lush blue where butterflies play,
A tiny tale spun from dawn to the day.
A beetle in boots struts with flair,
Claiming, "I'm off to deliver a dare!"

The daisies all giggle, their heads in a sway,
As the offbeat beetle rolls on his way.
He bumps into snails who are taking a break,
Crying, "What's the rush? Don't you love a good lake?"

With frogs in tuxedos who sing out of tune,
And fireflies twinkling beneath the full moon.
They gather for jokes around lily pad fires,
As chortles and chuckles keep raising the wires!

Tiny trees whisper their secrets so bright,
As the night dances on, twinkling with light.
In this world so small, each moment's a thrill,
Filled with laughter and joy, and a dash of goodwill!

Fables from the Forest Floor

In a meadow, a gopher grand,
Wore a crown of acorn and planned.
He claimed to be king of the ground,
With subjects like ants gathering round.

A squirrel with dreams of flight,
Built a rocket from leaves, what a sight!
He zoomed through the trees, such a fuss,
But landed in mud with a big, loud thuss!

A mouse sold tickets to a show,
Where beetles danced in a line, row by row.
They jived and spun, no end in sight,
Till a wind came through and shooed them in fright.

So remember the giggles in dirt,
Where tales rise up like the fun they hurt.
A forest of laughter, wide and sweet,
With stories to brighten each small critter's feet.

The Smallest Stories of Great Height

A tiny tree dreamed to touch the sky,
With branches so small, it let out a sigh.
But a bird named Lou, so full of glee,
Said, "I believe you'll grow, just wait and see!"

With whispers of wind, the little tree swayed,
While creatures below prepared their parade.
A hedgehog donned shoes, shiny and bright,
And danced 'neath the stars, what a peculiar sight!

A butterfly fluffed up her grandest best,
To show off her colors, like a jewel she dressed.
She flitted and fluttered, making quite the buzz,
While the little tree chuckled, "Oh, look at us!"

So remember this tale from a forest breeze,
Where giants are tiny and tales bring you fees.
Each story unique, every leaf a delight,
In heights or in depths, if shared, they're all right.

Echoes of Earthbound Enchantment

In a nook of the woods, where the shadows play,
A snail claimed he raced on the fastest of days.
While others just laughed at his slow, steady course,
He said, "Catch me, my friends, I'm a galloping horse!"

A rabbit with dreams of a carrot-filled feast,
Organized races that invited the beast.
But tripping on roots, he'd tumble and roll,
Laughing out loud at his bright, bouncy soul.

The crickets composed a soft, croaky tune,
While frogs leapt around in a groovy cartoon.
Yet a turtle, convinced he'd lead the grand show,
Took ages to warm up, moving oh-so-slow!

So listen close now to these charming walks,
Where creatures engage in the silliest talks.
With echoes of laughter beneath the old trees,
These roots hide the secrets of joy in the breeze.

Petites of the Ponderosa

A tiny pine sprouted beside a big oak,
Proclaiming, "I'm mighty!" with each little poke.
But the oak just chuckled, swaying for fun,
"Dear friend, you're cute, but I'm hard to outrun!"

On a rock, a ladybug threw a grand ball,
Inviting all critters, from big to small.
But the dance floor shook with each minuscule tap,
And ants used the leaves to form a great map.

A chipmunk named Charlie built a long slide,
From a branch to the ground, oh, what a ride!
But he zipped right off, landing soft in a ditch,
Crying, "What a thrill, but it gave me a twitch!"

So gather 'round now, hear these small sights,
Where groot encounters spark silly delights.
In the Ponderosa, remember with glee,
The whimsical wonders of life's jubilee.

The Wonders of Weathered Boughs

In a grove where the gnarled branches sway,
A wise old oak tells jokes all day.
Its bark is rough, but humor is bright,
Puns drift down like leaves in flight.

The willow weeps but adds a quip,
"I won't drown, I'm just on a trip!"
With each gust, their laughter entwines,
A comedy show of wrinkled designs.

The birch chimes in with a twist of fate,
"Why did the tree sit and wait?
To leaf the past behind, you see,
And branch out just as wild and free!"

As the sunset paints the skies so wide,
Boughs share tales of joy and pride.
In this forest, smiles always bloom,
Where every tree has room for humor's loom.

Dreams in the Dappled Light

Undercanopy, a squirrel's parade,
Chasing shadows, making mischief displayed.
Dreams dance like sunlight on furry cheeks,
Nutty laughter, in nature, it speaks.

A chipmunk dreams of a giant toast,
With berry jam, it's not a boast!
It flips and flops in dappled rays,
Creating jokes to brighten the days.

Each sunbeam whispers a secret, bold,
Of nuts and acorns and stories untold.
Rippling giggles on the forest floor,
Echoing tales that forever soar.

Dappled light plays tricks with sight,
As creatures join in joyous delight.
In this world where laughter grows,
Dreams skip and hop 'round roots, it knows.

Whispers of the Weenie Woods

In the Weenie Woods where things get wild,
A critter, small, yet humor is styled.
With acorns as hats, they frolic and play,
Tickled by breezes that dance and sway.

The tiny turtles tell tales of the rain,
"One drop broke my shell—what a pain!"
The giggles ring out, causing a scene,
As frogs leap about in grass that's green.

With mushrooms as tables, they share some soup,
Gossipy jays form a feathered troupe.
Every rustle and whisper brings forth a grin,
In the goofy woods, let the fun begin!

And as the sun casts its golden hue,
Creativity sparks and ideas brew.
From slumbering branches to roots underground,
The Weenie Woods echo vibrant sound.

Fables Beneath the Bowing Branches

Beneath the branches that bend and swoop,
A critter convention—a laugh-filled troop!
Tales of the wind and whoosh of the trees,
Whispering secrets shared by the breeze.

A fox struts by, with a jest up its sleeve,
"Ever heard of the tree that could weave?
It knit a sweater for winter's chill,
With branches all tangled, what a thrill!"

A wise old badger shares dreams of great schemes,
Of nut-stuffed feasts and soft mossy dreams.
With laughter that echoes through shadows and light,
Fables are spun till the fall of night.

As starlight twinkles through leaves that sway,
Each tale weaves a smile in its playful way.
Underneath these boughs, stories take flight,
In a world where whimsy reigns day and night.

Secrets of the Stunted Forest

In a forest so small, the squirrels conspire,
Making acorn pies that are covered in fire.
They dance on the leaves, beneath tiny moons,
And sing silly songs to the playful raccoons.

A wise little owl with his glasses askew,
Tells tales of the branches that always feel blue.
He hoots with delight, and the trees all just giggle,
As the gumdrops and twigs begin to do the wiggle.

The mushrooms grow tall, but they're only the height,
Of a very small mouse on a refrigerator night.
They laugh at the clouds, who are well out of range,
And share all their secrets with fairy-like change.

So if you should wander through this jolly place,
Look out for a leaf that can dance with great grace.
For the stunted trees host a comedy show,
Where the giggles of nature put on quite the glow.

Stories from the Stems

Once, a clever seed had a plan to take flight,
On a leaf-shaped rocket, it soared through the night.
But the wind had a laugh, and it blew with a shove,
Sending our sprout to the land of the dove.

The dandelions claim they can do a ballet,
Twisting and turning in a fanciful way.
While the grasses all giggle and sway to the beat,
Making sure that spring's dance is ever so sweet.

Tiny critters hold court, with mushrooms as seats,
Judging the bouncing of sad little beats.
The fern's a great singer, with notes so refined,
While the weeds play drums with their roots intertwined.

So listen real close when you stroll through the green,
The stories unfold that are silly but keen.
In stems where the laughter meets sunshine and dew,
The tiniest tales are the biggest for you.

Myths Amidst the Moss

Deep in the moss where the garden gnomes play,
They cook up a feast made of yesterday's hay.
The snails bring the butter and slugs bring the bread,
And the mushrooms all chuckle at what they have said.

A beetle declared he could fly like a bird,
But stumbled and tumbled, it was truly absurd.
His friends had a laugh, but he didn't feel blue,
He turned on their tunes with a jazzy bamboo.

A tiny fern whispers of trolls so small,
That they dance with the ants and do the grand crawl.
While the tadpoles conspire, plotting tricks on the breeze,

Turning dew drops to sprinkles, oh what a tease!

When the stars twinkle down on this magical patch,
The wild stories flow, as they huddle and hatch.
For in myths of the moss, where laughter runs free,
The tiniest wonders can spark joy like a spree.

Tales of the Diminutive Giants

In a land where the tiny have giant-sized dreams,
The berries agree on the best jelly themes.
They come to a party, each fruit's dressed to cheer,
With a sprinkle of glitter and giggles to share.

A little twig hero, with a cap made of bark,
Saves the day when the owls all miss the mark.
He tickles the feathers of sleepy old birds,
Turning troubles to laughter without any words.

The ants throw confetti, their dance is so grand,
While the grass blades all cheer, forming a band.
With each crooked note, the world sways with glee,
In a symphony made for the critters so free.

So gather 'round closely, and listen with glee,
To the tales of the giants, so lively and free.
For in the heart of the small, the biggest fun lies,
Where laughter and joy make the sweetest surprise.

The Legend of the Little Maple Leaf

In a garden so cozy, beneath the sun's beam,
Lived a maple leaf with a wild, wacky dream.
It wanted to fly, soar high in the air,
But it could only wiggle and giggle in despair.

With a gust from the breeze, it took to the sky,
Only to plop in a puddle nearby.
Yet it danced on the water, with splashes so sweet,
Every drop held a laugh, a silly retreat.

One day a squirrel thought it'd join in the fun,
But he slipped on the leaf and the splashes begun.
They both made a ruckus, a splashy encore,
Who knew such small things could cause such uproar?

Now the garden remembers the day they took flight,
When a leaf and a squirrel turned chaos to light.
With giggles and wiggles, they're legends, you see,
In a world full of wonder, as fun as can be.

Murmurs of the Meandering Vines

Deep in the forest where the wild things creep,
Lived playful green vines that were never quite steep.
They twisted and turned in a marvelous way,
Whispering secrets that brightened the day.

One vine named Vince, with a flair for a joke,
Would loop 'round a tree and pretend to be smoke.
It tickled the branches, and leaves roared with glee,
As they danced in the wind, in fanciful spree.

Then came a raccoon with a curious peek,
He tripped on the vines, "Oh dear, let me speak!"
"You vines are too silly, what's wrong with your mind?"
They giggled and swayed, leaving him quite confined.

Now whenever the sun casts a warm, golden ray,
The vines weave their stories, in fun, they will play.
With giggles and twists, they murmur and shine,
For laughter brings joy, like the best vintage wine.

Whims of the Wandering Woods

In the woods filled with giggles, the trees start to sway,
They concoct wild tales, in a whimsical way.
A pine called Petey wore a hat made of moss,
Claiming he was the king, but it made him look boss.

"Bow before me!" he chuckled, with pride in his bark,
As ferns curtsied deeply, a humorous lark.
But the wispy old willow, well-known for her sass,
Just rolled her green eyes and said, "What a farce!"

Then a group of brave rabbits jumped up with a cheer,
"We challenge the king to a hopping frontier!"
They leapt and they bounded, much faster than trees,
While the trunks watched in awe, swaying gently with ease.

Now Petey the Pine says humility's sweet,
As he shares his grand throne with the nimble, fleet feet.
In the woods full of humor, they laugh and unwind,
In the whimsical realm, where the fun's intertwined.

Echoes of the Elven Escapade

In the glens where the elves with their giggles reside,
They plotted a prank that they could not abide.
With mushrooms and flowers, they crafted a stew,
A potion that caused quite the fluster, it's true.

The leader, a fellow named Finn with a flair,
Proclaimed, "Let's see who can float in the air!"
So they drank from the brew, and up, they all flew,
Only to circle back and fall into dew.

They landed in laughter, all muddled and twirled,\nWith petals and acorns, their antics unfurled.
"We're flying, we're falling, we're totally free!"
They rolled in the grass, all knee-deep in glee.

Now each year, they gather, the elves bring a cheer,
To celebrate mischief, their favorite cheer.
With echoes of laughter, in the bright, golden light,
Their escapades sparkle, a pure, joyful sight.

The Wonders of the Weeping Willows

In the garden where the willows weep,
The squirrels gossip, oh what a heap.
A raccoon dances, to tunes so bright,
While the sun peeks through, a comical sight.

The branches sway like arms in a fight,
Shaking off raindrops with pure delight.
The frogs are crooning their silly songs,
In the shadows where every tree belongs.

A ladybug wears a dandy hat,
While the grasshoppers prance, imagine that!
The roots hold secrets, tales they know well,
Of a woodland party, where critters dwell.

So next time you stroll by these leafy friends,
Remember their giggles, the joy never ends.
Weeping willows don't just sigh and bend,
They're the life of the party, your laughter they send.

Joys of the Diminutive Grove

In a grove so small, with trees that giggle,
A hedgehog spins while the owls all wiggle.
The ferns are lush, like pillows of green,
Every breeze whispers, "Come have a scene!"

Acorn hats are worn with great pride,
By tiny ants who take a joyride.
The mushrooms are chefs, cooking with flair,
Creating stews that they joyfully share.

A mouse in a cloak, oh what a sight,
Sells tiny wares from morning till night.
The sunbeams giggle as shadows play,
In the grove full of laughter, bright as the day.

So frolic around in this jolly place,
Join in the fun, let smiles take place.
For in this small grove, big hearts do sing,
Celebrating life's joys, oh what joy they bring!

The Treetop Dreamers

High up in the branches, where dreams take flight,
The bubbles that float make a whimsical sight.
A sloth on a leaf is stuck in a nap,
While a squirrel plays trumpets from his funny lap.

The stars in the night, they twinkle and gleam,
As owls tell stories that burst like a dream.
Raccoons wear pajamas, all snug and tight,
While the tree frogs hop in a dance of delight.

Bright fireflies flicker, like tiny lamps,
They twirl through the air, in joyful camps.
The tree trunks are canvases of tales spun bright,
With graffiti of laughter beneath the moonlight.

So listen closely to the branches that sway,
They whisper of tales, of frolicsome play.
In the treetops above, where dreamers take pause,
Life's a merry jest, let's all give applause!

Echoes from the Tiny Groves

In the tiny groves, where shadows prance,
The flowers gossip, they know how to dance.
A butterfly flips, a twirl and a spin,
While ladybugs cheer, inviting you in.

The crickets compose their nighttime tune,
A melody sweet under the glowing moon.
With whispers of secrets carried on the breeze,
Nature's humor sways in the gentle trees.

There's giggling grass, with a tickle or two,
As chipmunks play peek-a-boo, oh so true.
The twigs stand up straight like soldiers on guard,
Guarding the laughter, not very hard!

So wander on in, let your heart sing free,
In the tiny groves, where joy's a decree.
With each chuckle shared, and every smile wide,
Echoes of fun in nature's great ride!

Tales of the Petite Pinecones

In a forest so snug, where the shadows play,
A pinecone once dreamed of a grand cabaret.
With acorn musicians and a squirrel ballet,
They danced in the moonlight till the break of day.

A princess of twigs wore a crown made of moss,
She pranced on the stage, she was never at loss.
The whispers of wind gave her royal gloss,
While chipmunks applauded, their tiny limbs cross.

The laughter erupted, the joy filled the air,
As raindrops turned flush and brought giggles to flair.
They twirled and they leapt without any care,
In the heart of the woods, a stage rare and rare.

And when dawn arrived, with a yawn and a stretch,
Each tiny performer had joy to sketch.
They promised to meet, and they made a new sketch,
Of laughter and fun that they'd never forget.

Stories from the Undersized Oaks

In a grove where the sunbeams would barely ignite,
Two oaks, both so small, had plans for a night.
With acorns for cups, they made cider delight,
They laughed till they toppled, what a whimsical sight!

The mushrooms brought snacks, and the beetles made beats,
While worms wiggled under, as they tap-danced on seats.
The owls traded tales, and the crickets had feats,
Of heroes from gardens and runaway sweets.

Then came the wise fox, with a grin ear to ear,
He spun funny yarns, yet made all of them cheer.
With stories of mischief and fish without fear,
The night became magic, their worries unclear.

At dawn, they'd reflected, their hearts all aglow,
These tiny oak wonders, with friendships that grow.
In the shade of their branches, a joyful tableau,
Of laughter and whispers, they'd forever bestow.

The Lore of the Littlest Trees

In the meadow so bright, with flowers a-flutter,
Lived tiny tree saplings, each one a cute utter.
With dreams slightly lofty and hearts that are utter,
They plotted to grow up, but first, a fun clutter.

One day they decided to throw a grand feast,\nWith
dandelion cakes that would baffle the beast.
The ants brought the drinks, while the bees made the yeast,
It turned into madness, but joy, never ceased.

They danced in their roots, while the grass sang along,
With shimmery petals that twinkled like song.
The shadows got jealous, and the wind grew a strong,
But their laughter and cheer just kept growing all wrong.

At sunset they promised to never grow tall,
For being the littlest was fun after all.
Their tales would be whispered where everyone's small,
In a space where each giggle was big and not small.

Fables Written in Fern Fronds

In a patch of green whisper, where shy ferns sway,
Lived creatures of charm who would frolic and play.
With tiny leaf scrolls, they'd map every way,
And twist their tall tales, come what may.

A hedgehog named Henry wrote poems so bright,
Of knights clad in cobwebs, who danced in the night.
The snails did a ballet, setting all things right,
While ladybugs laughed, what a whimsical sight!

Beneath the soft layers of fern fronds so low,
The whispers of stories began to flow.
With laughter erupting and a magical glow,
They feasted on dreams that forever would grow.

And as sunlight dimmed, with a wink and a cheer,
They gathered together, casting aside fear.
For in fables of ferns, their laughter was clear,
The magic of friendship was always so near.

Narratives of the Nestled Roots

In a tiny thicket, a squirrel took flight,
Chasing a shadow, mistaken for night.
A pinecone proclaimed, "I'm the fairest here!"
While the dandelions giggled, we've nothing to fear.

A hamster once claimed he could jump to the moon,
But tripped on a twig and sang a sad tune.
The sunflowers laughed, sporting petals like hats,
As the worm donned a cape, striking heroic spats.

The mushrooms held court, with a frog as the king,
His throne made of leaves, oh, what a fine thing!
They feasted on raindrops, the juice of the rain,
While the beetles exchanged tales, and danced in the grain.

Underneath ferns, the wise owls convened,
Challenging beavers to build and to glean.
With laughter they carved out stories so grand,
Of the tiny trees dreaming of castles in sand.

A Few Inches of Wonder

A tiny frog hopped on a leaf of the brook,
Claiming it led to a magical nook.
He whispered to crickets, "The world's not so small,"
While a snail laughed aloud, "There's room for us all!"

The beetles put on a theatrical play,
Starring a spider who lost his ballet.
They twirled and they spun, on a twig of fine grace,
While the ants rolled their eyes, but still joined the race.

Each acorn a dreamer, with wishes to share,
Believing one day they could grow into air.
The roots spread wide, though they never grew tall,
In a world of their own, there was room for them all.

The blossoms all chuckled, with dance moves so bright,
As petals spilled laughter through the softening light.
With whispers of wonders, they twinkled and twirled,
In a universe small, overflowing with worlds.

Oak Dreams in an Acorn World

In a playground of leaves, acorns cultivated dreams,
Each one a giant, or so it seems.
With plans for high castles, and marshmallow queens,
While busy little ants stitched their cool jean seams.

A ladybug signed up for the talent show,
Juggling dewdrops with flair, putting on a show.
The grasshoppers chirped, "You've got quite the flair!"
While the moon peeked down, bemused in the air.

The tallest of tales spread in whispers of dew,
Where clouds played charades and the sun called it true.
A revelry of jesters, all tiny in height,
Laughed under starry blankets, deep into the night.

As crickets composed symphonies, soft on the breeze,
The roots hummed along, a chorus with ease.
In this small but grand realm, together they'd sway,
Creating big dreams on a bright, sunny day.

Folklore from the Forgotten Glade

In a glade full of giggles, where shadows align,
A hedgehog recited his favorite line.
"It's not how you grow, but the fun that we take,
From stories of magic, and baked berry cake!"

With mushrooms as tables, and dew drops for cheer,
The critters convened, celebrating their fear.
"Tell me of giants," squeaked a shy little mouse,
"Or the day when the toads had an alligator's house!"

So off went the stories that leaped through the air,
Of a snail with a hat, and a pig with a chair.
The whispers of laughter grew louder and clearer,
In the forest of fables, nothing could be dearer.

Under the bright moon, they danced on a whim,
Believing in wonders, their eyes growing dim.
With the tales of the trees weaving magic so straight,
In a world so fantastical, they cherished their fate.

Quests of the Pint-Size Pines

A tiny pine plotted a grand escape,
With acorn helmets, they formed a brave troupe.
They marched through the grass, so bold and so spry,
While ants cheered them on, as they passed by.

They sought out the winds that swayed high above,
But each gust would toss them, like pawns in a shove.
They tumbled and giggled, in laughter they soared,
A mischief of pines, by adventure adored.

At the top of their hill, they found little snacks,
A feast fit for giants, with no plans to relax.
With berries for dinner, they danced 'neath the stars,
These pint-sized adventurers, the kings of their bars.

So raise up a cheer, for the glee they unfold,
For little things know great tales, that never get old.
Each whimsy-filled journey, a tale worth retelling,
In laughter, they thrive, with their joy ever swelling.

The Preserved Dreams of Twisted Stems

In a garden where misfits grew wild and free,
Stems twisted and turned, chatting 'neath a tree.
With dreams of the skies, they plotted with glee,
To dance in the breeze and sip cupfuls of tea.

A gnarled stem declared, "Let's fly really high!"
But first, we must find a way to the sky.
They fashioned a ladder from sticks and some leaves,
And their hopes soared up, like warm air through eaves.

Each step up the rungs made them giggle and clap,
"I'm a bird! No, a plane! Wait, it's just a mishap!"
They fluttered and flopped, like a kite in a snare,
Twisted and tangled, but none felt a care.

So dream on, dear stems, with your peculiar schemes,
As every wild twist is alive with dreams.
In laughter, you'll find how to twist fate around,
In the charm of the crazy, true joy will be found.

The Symphony of Small Boughs

In a grove where the small boughs played tunes with delight,
They strummed on their branches, from morning till night.

With chirps and with rustles, they formed a grand band,
Each note full of mischief, each beat just so grand.

The saplings would sway to the rhythm of time,
While critters danced close with an acorn on mime.
Their concert was wild, with a cacophony pure,
For laughter was music, the kind that endures.

With twigs for the drumsticks and berries for bells,
They rocked out the tunes, as the earth sang its spells.
A woodpecker joined in, with taps and with claps,
The whole forest joined in, in a symphonic lap.

So bump up the tempo, let the gaiety swell,
For joy in small woods, oh can't you just tell?
In the symphony played, every sigh turns to cheer,
For even the smallest can have a grand year.

Revelations from the Hidden Glade

In a glade tucked away where the ferns like to chat,
Stood secrets and whispers, all snug in a mat.
From berries that giggled, to mushrooms that spun,
Each secret so silly, a mystery for fun.

A squirrel came prancing, with tales to relay,
Of dreams he had chased through the last sunny day.
But tripping on roots, with a dizzied surprise,
He flipped in a circle, then rolled with the sighs.

The flowers looked on, with a giggling glee,
"A squirrel's just a cat when he dances like me!"
And so they all burst, into fits of delight,
For secrets are better when shared with a bite.

So in this lush glade, where humor prevails,
Every flutter and frond has its own funny tales.
In laughter, we find where our dreams twine and roam,
In secrets revealed, everyone feels at home.

Whispers of the Woodland

In the depths of the wood, where the squirrels parade,
A chipmunk once danced, in a nut-fitting shade.
He boasted of acorns, as big as balloons,
But slipped on a twig, singing off tune.

A rabbit in bowties told tales of great fights,
With shadows of owls that soared in the nights.
He hopped with such flair, but was caught in a thicket,
The hero of snacks, but forgot how to pick it.

The trees leaned in close, with a chuckle so deep,
As the badger made claims of the dreams that he keeps.
He swore he could fly, with a cape made of bark,
But ended up lost, on a stroll in the park.

With giggles and grins, the forest was bright,
As stories took flight in the heart of the night.
The littlest creatures, with dreams oh so grand,
Twirled in their tales, hand in fluffy hand.

Legends Beneath the Canopy

Beneath the tall branches, in shadows they reign,
A hedgehog spun yarns of riches and fame.
He claimed he was king of a treasure so bold,
But his jewels turned out to be just bits of old gold.

A fox with a wink shared his plans full of zeal,
To outsmart a bear with a grand spinning wheel.
But he tripped on a root, and rolled down a hill,
Leaving laughter in waves, and a tale to fulfill.

The raccoons held court, 'neath the moon's silver glow,
As they swapped all their stories, both clever and slow.
They giggled and guffawed with each twist of their fate,
As legends grew larger, it's never too late.

In this bustling grove, every beast had a plot,
With hiccups and snickers, they laughed a whole lot.
From tiny tall tales, under twilight's embrace,
The laughter of nature fills each little space.

Chronicles of the Little Saplings

Tiny saplings stood straight, with courage to boast,
Of giants they met, on their leap and their toast.
A tiny tree claimed it once touched the sky,
But the wind blew it down, oh my, oh my!

The mushrooms conspired, with hats on their heads,
As they munched on the stories of greens and the reds.
One boasted of clouds, made of candy so sweet,
But feared getting stuck in a sugary treat.

A ladybug swirled with her spotty, fine grace,
She danced on a leaf, in a curious place.
With each twirl she spun, new legends took flight,
Of adventures she had in the warm summer light.

From all corners of bushes, they gathered in glee,
Unraveling tales as fun as can be.
The chronicles kept growing, as stories ran wide,
From little saplings sprouted, with laughter as their guide.

Giant Dreams in Miniature Leaves

In a garden so small, where the gnomes keep their dreams,

A beetle in boots told of gold for the teams.
He whispered of riches, tucked under a stone,
But tripled his stories each time he was prone.

The ladybirds laughed at a mouse full of pride,
Who claimed he could swim on a leaf for a ride.
He jumped in the pond, but alas, what a splash!
Now he tells tales of his brave, little crash.

A shadow of cloud laughed at all that it saw,
As squirrels held court with a nutty old law.
They claimed every seed could grow fortunes anew,
But first, they must dig with their brand new shoe crew.

As dusk settled in, and the stars took their place,
Each creature shared laughs in this comical space.
With dreams intertwined, they spun tales so bright,
Of giant adventures beneath the moonlight.

Myths from the Mossy Kingdom

In a kingdom where mushrooms dance,
Frogs wear crowns and take a chance.
Whispers of spiders weave their threads,
Telling tales where snails earn beds.

A squirrel claims he's the king of flight,
Riding on the back of a blushing sprite.
While ants plan feats of flight and cheer,
But in the end, they just bring beer.

The owls boast of wisdom, oh so grand,
Yet forget where they dropped their brand.
With tangled branches, they can't see clear,
Mistaking twigs for a tiny deer.

In this mossy realm, laughter replays,
As critters enjoy their silly bays.
From fables spun in the thick of night,
Mirth grows tall out of nature's sight.

Journeys of the Leafy Dreams

A leaf set sail on a breeze so sweet,
Waving goodbye to its tree-y seat.
It dreamed of adventures both wild and grand,
But landed slap on a picnic stand.

The ants threw a party with crumbs galore,
While the leaf tried to swab the mess from the floor.
But it slipped and it slid, creating a mess,
All the critters agreed, "What a leafy jest!"

A ladybug rode it like a bold knight,
Challenging winds to join in the flight.
Yet gusts tangled dreams in a twist of fate,
The leaf laughed hard, saying, "I'm late!"

In dreams that dance from branch to limb,
Stories of fun and laughter brim.
With every flutter and playful gleam,
In leafy realms, it's a wild-themed dream.

The Heights of Humble Seeds

Humble seeds with dreams so grand,
Hoped to grow into a mighty band.
But sprouted low, they poked their heads,
And giggled loud from their soft bed.

One claimed to reach the clouds so high,
While another just wanted to wave goodbye.
But roots entangled, in jest they bickered,
And at the sun, they shyly snickered.

"We're destined to stretch and be well known,
To grow like giants, in time we've grown!"
Yet squirrels scampered, taking their cues,
And whispered secrets of their tiny blues.

In the quiet of soil, above the ground,
They plot their fun, just spinning around.
For in every seed, there's a tale so spry,
Of dreams that dance beneath the sky.

Tiny Legends Beneath the Canopy

Beneath the leaves, a world unknown,
Tales of critters in mischief grown.
Bugs who wear hats made of flowers bright,
Frolicking under the soft moonlight.

A mouse claimed to hunt giant cheese,
While the snails just took it with ease.
With tales of giants that never did come,
The laughter erupted, oh so fun!

A caterpillar donned a superhero cape,
Saving the day with a loop and a scrape.
The butterflies blushed and flitted with glee,
Dreaming of futures, oh so carefree.

In this leafy realm, stories do bloom,
Where every critter escapes from their gloom.
Beneath the canopy, joy takes flight,
Tiny legends thrive, oh what a sight!

www.ingramcontent.com/pod-product-compliance
Lightning Source LLC
Chambersburg PA
CBHW071825160426
43209CB00003B/208